jillian potashnick

the 5

f-bombs

and our attempts at defusing them

The 5 F-Bombs

and our attempts at defusing them

Jillian Potashnick

BALBOA.
PRESS

A DIVISION OF HAY HOUSE

Balboa Press books may be ordered through booksellers or by contacting:

Balboa Press
A Division of Hay House
1663 Liberty Drive
Bloomington, IN 47403
www.balboapress.com
1 (877) 407-4847

Because of the dynamic nature of the Internet, any web addresses or links contained in this book may have changed since publication and may no longer be valid. The views expressed in this work are solely those of the author and do not necessarily reflect the views of the publisher, and the publisher hereby disclaims any responsibility for them.

The author of this book does not dispense medical advice or prescribe the use of any technique as a form of treatment for physical, emotional, or medical problems without the advice of a physician, either directly or indirectly. The intent of the author is only to offer information of a general nature to help you in your quest for emotional and spiritual well-being. In the event you use any of the information in this book for yourself, which is your constitutional right, the author and the publisher assume no responsibility for your actions.

Interior Image Credit: Evelyn Bark

Print information available on the last page.

ISBN: 978-1-9822-3252-8 (sc)
ISBN: 978-1-9822-3253-5 (hc)
ISBN: 978-1-9822-3254-2 (e)

Library of Congress Control Number: 2019911250

Balboa Press rev. date: 08/07/2019

To Eric, Leo, and all my extended family for their continued support of my crazy shenanigans, and to all of my best girlfriends (past, present, and future) who've helped encourage me to be exactly who I am.

Namaste.

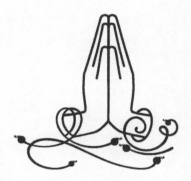

Contents

introduction

***

OH, HI THERE!

Over a glass of wine (or three), my friends and I would find ourselves discussing the exact same topics that I've been hearing my fitness clients vent about for years. They all revolve around the constant female struggles I have affectionately labeled "the five F-bombs"—food, fitness, friends, family, and faith. Much like a seesaw, life has its ups, downs, and fun times along the way, no matter our age. This childhood playground pastime requires a combination of work, resistance, and balance, which actually relates to our everyday lives, and we never even knew it.

Have you found yourself wondering things like:

- *What the hell am I going to make for dinner tonight?*
  Food bomb
  o   Not mac-n-cheese again!

- *How do I get motivated to fit back into my designer jeans?*
  Fitness bomb
  o   They were an "investment" after all.

- *I need to find my new adult girl-gang.*
  Friend bomb
  o   You're never too old for a BFF!

- *I'm trying to define my current family roles.*
  Family bomb
  o   Um, pass the Xanax, please.

- *If there really is a God, why does chocolate taste so good and brussels sprouts taste so bad?*
  Faith bomb
  o   The world may never know!

If you can relate to having had any of these thoughts cross your mind, and I know you can, then this book is definitely for you. I have spent over a decade working in the fitness industry, training women between thirty and seventy years of age. While that may sound like a pretty big age range, what I discovered was that we are all struggling with the same F-bombs on an almost daily basis. This is not a how-to book, as there isn't only one way to defuse any of these bombs. It is merely a collection of stories, suggestions, and ideas that, like an all-you-can-eat Vegas buffet, you can add to your plate or pass right on by. *The Five F-Bombs* will take you on a lighthearted, humorous, and informative journey through the commonalities that women share and discuss with their female counterparts when working out or hanging out. You will laugh, you may cry, and hopefully you will even learn something cool along the way. Let the fun begin!

chapter 1

FOOD BOMB

Whether you're shopping for groceries, preparing a meal, choosing a snack, dining out, debating over dessert, socializing at happy hour, or getting a kid to take three more bites, when it comes to food, quantity and quality are probably on the forefront of your mind, even if only momentarily. As they should be! Food is the primary fuel to your most prized possession—your body. You literally can't go anywhere without it. You fill it with caffeine in the morning, water throughout the day, maybe an adult libation at night, and hope you don't run out of gas before getting to watch an uninterrupted hour of Netflix before turning in for the night. Do you fill up on premium, unleaded, regular, or diesel? Either way, it all starts with accumulating information, devising a plan, and knowing your budget.

The Dreaded Weekly Trip to the Grocery Store

I don't know about you, but I absolutely hate the task of grocery shopping. I mean, I really despise it. Everything from making a list of all the things to buy, then driving to the store, avoiding rogue shopping carts in the parking lot, remembering to grab the reusable bags from the trunk, and finding the least sticky cart to push up and down the chilly, retail-filled aisles makes me want to pull my hair out. There isn't a single aspect of this that appeals to me in any way. Do I fall for the "buy two, get one free" promotion? Absolutely, every time, guilty as charged! And usually without regard for where I'm going to store them or expiration dates. But before I call it quits, I look into the cart and ask myself these questions:

- Are there foods that pair well together?
  If not, back it up and grab its partner in crime. After all, no one can use the guacamole without something to put it on.

- Can I spot all the colors of the rainbow?
  If not, find more fruits or veggies to fill in the gaps. It's a fun game to play if you're shopping with kids in tow.

- If I ran into someone I knew right now, would I be embarrassed by anything in my cart?
  If so, remove those items immediately. Yes, the Twinkies are definitely a bad idea.

Finally circling back to the front of the store (yet again), I'm ready to check out. Now it's time for the thrilling, high-stakes game of picking the right lane, which is always a gamble. Do I go with the chatty cashier whose line is shorter, or the quick cashier whose line is longer? "Six of one, half dozen of the other," as my mom would say. Unloading the contents of the shopping cart onto the conveyor belt is almost like doing a walk of shame. Are people judging me right now? I can feel their eyes scanning my purchases. Then, watching the math quickly add up on the bottom of the screen is always alarming, and I find myself wishing I had paid more attention in math class. The filled-to-the-brim reusable bags make their way into my cart like a skillful game of Tetris, and I'm off to the car… if only I could remember where I parked it. I find myself loading the trunk with great speed, and running to the cart-return and back because I still need to go home to unload the car before anything melts.

First, I put the freezer items quickly into the freezer, then the refrigerated food finds its way into the fridge, and lastly, the dry goods and toiletries get distributed to their proper shelves. Phew, mission completed! And guess what will likely happen after all of this? My family will open the fridge or pantry, stare blankly into the abyss, and say, "We have nothing to eat."

Look at the bottom of your receipt the next time you do your weekly shopping to see how many items you bought. Efficient grocery shopping is (unfortunately) not something they teach us in school. So it's no wonder so many of us feel like we're lost in a never-ending labyrinth of bright lights, false advertising, and impulse buys.

As someone who doesn't like to cook but still has to eat and provide nutritional food for her family, what's a woman to do? I have devised a shopping list of twenty items, in five different categories, to buy that can be used interchangeably to make different quick, healthy, and delicious meals in less than fifteen minutes. By simply swapping out the veggies or protein used when repeating the recipe, it will change both the flavor profile and aesthetic of the dish.

sample grocery list

fruits
Avocados
Berries
Cucumbers
Squash

veggies
Asparagus
Bell peppers
Red Onions
Zucchini

starch
Brown Rice
Couscous
Quinoa
Tortillas

protein
Chicken
Edamame
Eggs
Salmon

toppings
Feta Cheese
Hummus
Salsa
Shredded Lettuce

Breakfast of Champions
Scrambled eggs with fresh veggies, feta cheese, and sliced avocado. Seasonal berries on the side.

Rainbow Lunch Wrap
Spread hummus onto a whole wheat tortilla to act as the glue. Then cover the hummus with chopped bell peppers, cucumbers, red onions, feta cheese, and shredded lettuce.

Easy-Peasy Dinner Protein Bowl
Start with a bowl of organic brown rice or couscous.
Pick a protein: salmon, chicken, or steamed edamame.
Add one chopped (grilled) bell pepper or zucchini.
Cover with your favorite salsa and sliced avocado.

Sunny Quinoa Anytime Bowl
1/2 cup cooked quinoa
3 teaspoons chopped cucumber
3 teaspoons chopped red onions
Sprinkle basil, dill, and feta cheese.
Place a sunny-side-up egg on top.
Add table salt and pepper to taste.

This can be done with any twenty ingredients that you choose. Just make sure you have at least three items from each of the five categories in order to create some variety. Gather a variety of recipes by utilizing the cookbooks you already have that are collecting dust in your home, making a food board on Pinterest, or following your favorite food bloggers. Be on the lookout for the main ingredients you want to incorporate that week. Do a quick Google search of your favorite ingredients that will provide plenty of recipes to choose from. The list provided above is just an example, as everyone's dietary restrictions are unique, and taste buds will vary from person to person. Remember to be creative and at the same time, keep it simple. It sounds like an oxymoron, I know. But this will help keep the family meals fresh, low stress, and on budget. As a time saver, you can make and refrigerate the starches on Sunday night to have handy all week. Protein can be cooked in batches and will stay good in the fridge for a few days.

Although research is always changing, and a printed book does not provide you with the luxury of constantly being updated, here are some interesting facts about our grocery shopping habits in the United States, according to extensive research compiled for a blog posted on StartUp-Port.com:

- The average shopping trip takes about forty-one minutes.
- More than 40 percent of shoppers say they go to more than one store to get everything they need.
- Sixty-nine percent of women say they make a list before going shopping.
- Shoppers hit the supermarket an average of one and a half times a week.
- The average weekly shopping bill in the US comes to $118.
- Among primary shoppers for households, 70 percent are women.
- Nearly 25 percent of the grocery bill is spent on processed foods and sweets.

Let this information spark conversations with you and your friends to see where you fall among the national average. The best place to learn tips and tricks is from your peers. Who you spend the most time with is likely going to be someone with a similar lifestyle, age, and income as you. You may be spending extra time and money unnecessarily and not even know it.

Top Three Tips on Avoiding Extra Calories throughout the Day

Yes, you can be amazing at grocery shopping, outstanding at food prep, and smart when dining out, but those little times before, in between, and after meals can still trip you up.

- Always have a bottle of water by your bed while you're sleeping, in your hand (or purse) when running errands, in the cup holder of your car, or while sitting at your desk. Basically, there should be fresh water within arm's reach at any given time of the day. You can't fill up on something that's not in front of your face. If you wait to drink water until you're parched, it's too late! You've probably already started confusing your thirst for hunger pangs, which leads to unnecessary snacking.

- As soon as you're finished eating your meal, pop in a piece of sugar-free gum or an after-dinner mint (as a palate cleanser) to signal your brain that you're done eating. Plus, whatever you were eating is not going to taste as good with mint flavor on your tongue. Who doesn't remember being a kid and accidentally drinking orange juice right after brushing your teeth? Gross! The same concept applies to stop yourself from getting a second (or third) helping.

- Only eat at the table and turn off the screens. When you're eating or snacking in the car, on the iPad, while texting, or watching TV, you will almost always end up consuming more calories. Naturally, your brain is preoccupied with where to turn next or what's happening on the show and is not able to fully focus on what you're putting in your mouth. Sitting at a table with minimal distractions allows you to practice the long-lost art of conversation and mindful eating. Using all of your senses can be enjoyable—smelling the food, seeing the variety of colors, tasting the flavors, experiencing the different textures or temperatures, even just listening to something sizzling. It will inevitably slow you down and allow you to feel full when you're actually full, so you won't overeat.

Healthy Snacking Is Possible

When you're suddenly hangry, here are a few ways to avoid grabbing the secret stash of Girl Scout cookies from your freezer. You know, the ones that are strategically hidden behind the bag of peas that you only bought for emergency head bumps. I mean, hey, the cookies are only sold once a year; those boxes need to last!

- Keep hard-boiled eggs already deshelled in the fridge for a quick high-protein fix. Eliminating the extra step of peeling the egg will remove an obstacle in a time crunch.

- Place small bowls of unsalted mixed nuts in various rooms of the house, so there's no need to wander into the kitchen where there are more options to choose from. Count out about ten or twelve and walk away, eating them slowly.

- After coming home from the grocery store, immediately rinse off and cut up any seasonal fruit (such as blueberries and strawberries), pluck the grapes off the vines, and combine them into several small plastic baggies. This makes it easy to grab fresh fruit from the fridge when you need a snack to throw in your bag before leaving the house.

- String cheese is high in calcium, fun to peel, requires no prep work or clean up, has a lengthy shelf life if refrigerated properly, and can be eaten on the go.

- Pistachio nuts provide a satisfying textural crunch for a healthy snack option and are a great source of B vitamins. Since they require so much effort to open, they take longer to consume; therefore, you will likely stop eating them once your hunger pang has passed. Side effects may include sore thumbs and a big mess to clean up!

Dining Out

There are some incredible local and chain restaurants where it absolutely is possible to enjoy a nice meal out and leave feeling satisfied but not stuffed. Even Taco Bell now offers a high-protein "Cantina" menu, a low-calorie "Fresco" menu, and a vegetarian menu!

- To find local mom-and-pop restaurants, either while at home or when traveling, I like to use the Yelp app for suggestions and tips. Just type "healthy food" in the search bar at the top. The first few will be sponsored ads, but thanks to a lengthy Q&A algorithm, the rest are recommended by actual Yelp users as having healthy options.

- Any chain restaurant that has a calorie count next to each item is going to be more health conscious than those who don't display it loud and proud on the menu. Panera Bread, California Pizza Kitchen, Chick-fil-A, Subway, Cheesecake Factory, Jason's Deli, and Chipotle are some that practice this concept. Instead of calorie counting, just try being calorie conscious instead. You have to make a choice anyway, so let this be the deciding factor.

- Say, "No thank you," if you see the server walking toward the table with a complimentary bread basket or bottomless chips and salsa. Once it's down, the temptation can be brutal. Save yourself the stress and calories by saying no in advance.

- Always ask for your salad dressing on the side, so that you are the one in control of the saturation amount. That's where the majority of the calories in salads are usually hiding.

Have Your Cake and Eat It Too

Dinner without dessert may feel like an unresolved movie ending that leaves you high and dry. You've invested two and a half hours of your life into these characters, and you want closure, damnit! Dessert is often looked at as the closure to a good meal. It's the fairy-tale ending that leaves you feeling all warm and fuzzy inside. Dinner is the last chance of the day to sit back and break bread with friends or family, and dessert is a great way to prolong that experience.

At school, at work, and at home, a birthday is a great excuse to bring people together to honor someone for basically breathing air for the last 365 days and enjoy a sweet treat to celebrate. Cupcakes, cookies, ice cream, and cake are big moneymakers in the pastry industry for this very reason. A close runner-up is the day loved ones say, "I do." Instead of depriving yourself from participating in celebratory occasions such as birthdays and weddings, where dessert is predetermined, say yes, but only put half of the piece on your plate, or share the full piece with a friend. The majority of the time, however, you do get a say in your dessert decision, so next time, try out some of these options:

- At a restaurant, the best low-cal (but still flavorful) option on the menu is usually going to be a bowl of fresh seasonal fruit. You can even add a scoop of sorbet.

- After dinner at home, for a sweet tooth craving, break off a few pieces of high-quality dark chocolate (70 percent cocoa or higher) to hit the spot.

- When entertaining kids, buy the mini premade vanilla ice-cream cones dipped in chocolate. They don't require cutting, forks, or plates and are a big hit!

Cheers! L'chaim! Salute!

If you want to cut calories fast, the obvious answer is always going to be to stop drinking any alcohol, period. It's no secret that alcoholic beverages are chock-full of sugar and empty calories. But for a lot of people, a glass of wine (or insert your preferred beverage of choice here) is something you might enjoy in the evenings, in moderation, and with good company. It could be what you most look forward to after your responsibilities at work or home are complete for the day, when celebrating a special occasion, or as a reward for finishing a difficult task. As an adult, you legally have the right to make that choice.

There is, however, a problem if you're drinking and then getting behind the wheel, showing up for work, saying or doing unkind things to your friends or loved ones, or regularly drinking to the point of blacking out. These are behaviors of drinking that I simply cannot support you on. You might need help, like yesterday. You also want to avoid the negative health risks associated with overdrinking, such as poor sleep, hypertension, liver damage, hormone imbalances, pancreatic complications, and potential for alcohol abuse and addiction. If you think you may struggle with this, please skip this section and go right to "Pizza Party!"

If that's *not* you, however, then welcome to the "OMG, it's five o'clock—my kids are still alive—I survived another day—I need a glass of wine" club! I'm a card-carrying member. Don't judge! The golden rule here is the same concept as food consumption: low quantity and high quality. Much like our undergarments, not all wine is created equal. But don't worry. I've salivated, I mean slaved, over the Riedel glassware to do the hard-hitting research so that you can reap all the benefits. You are welcome!

Did you know that there's more to a glass of red wine than meets the lips? It's true. Each glass carries a delightful blend of healthy plant-based chemicals that your body actually craves—yes, craves. Antioxidants, flavonoids, and polyphenols do a lot more than just make you feel relaxed and buzzed!

- Antioxidants play an important role in our body's ability to identify, tackle, and manage cell-damaging free radicals. In red wine specifically, the antioxidants' capabilities boost our immune system and lessen many harmful cell interactions.

- Flavonoids come from the seed and skin of the grape. They are the largest type of antioxidant found in red wine and also the healthiest. Woot-woot! Wine and flavonoids can lower blood pressure by helping to relax arteries and prevent cell stress.

- Polyphenols help reduce inflammation, improve artery function, lower cholesterol, and lower the chance of platelet clumps. Polyphenols are also found in some spices and dark chocolate with 70 percent or higher cocoa. Um, yes please!

"Red, Red Wine Makes Me Feel so Fine"
-UB40

According to Marketview Liquor's latest research (blog posted on May 3, 2018), when consumed in moderation (about five ounces a day for the average woman), red wine can, in fact, improve your overall heart health. If you have high blood pressure or high cholesterol, then it's true; you can benefit from the three compounds (listed above) that are found in most red wines. These compounds work together to reduce the bad cholesterol and encourage the good cholesterol. The top varietals that provide the best health benefits are as follows:

- **Malbec**
  These grapes have some of the thickest skins of all wine grapes, so maybe we women need to take a cue from them! They grow best in a particularly dense soil with less sulfate, positively affecting Malbec's smooth taste and health benefits.

- **Pinot Noir**
  These grapes begin their fermentation with some of the lowest amounts of natural sugar. This results in a lower calorie count per glass and lower overall sugar levels. This makes pinot noir a great choice for those of us watching our sugar intake.

- **Cabernet Sauvignon**
  These grapes are the most planted wine grapes in the world, taking up vineyard residency in more than eight hundred thousand acres across our beautiful planet—which is pretty smart, considering its many neural cell health benefits.

However, if wine is not your jam (pun intended), then here are some delicious low-cal liquor suggestions, courtesy of Yelena @cocktail_ vision to try out:

Oh Sweet Pea
1.5 ounces Empress Gin
half ounce Pavan Liquor
half ounce Lime Juice
a splash of soda water

Birdie Rose Gimlet
1.5 ounces Tito's Vodka
half ounce Rose Liquor
half ounce lime juice
a splash of soda water

Always drink responsibly, and be sure to eat food when you do.

Pizza Party!

Now that the drinks are taken care of, a guaranteed crowd pleaser when entertaining a group of people is pizza. Both young and old, it's always a fan favorite. Just be sure to pair it with a large colorful salad with various dressing options. In fact, I love pizza so much that one summer when I was nine years old, I challenged myself to only eat pizza for an entire week. Looking back, I can't imagine why my mom allowed me to attempt such a goal (she probably didn't think I would stick with it), but she didn't stop me, and I achieved it with flying colors! If you are craving pizza, don't deprive yourself. Just do it smartly and work from the bottom (the crust) on up to the toppings.

- **Crust**
  Luckily, in this day and age, places like Costco, California Pizza Kitchen, and Trader Joe's make or sell a cauliflower crust pizza that is out-of-this-world delicious. Seriously, you must try it! Practically every single pizza place now offers a gluten-free crust, if that's your tummy's desire. However, if you insist on eating your carbs, and I do, then thin crust is always a better option than hand tossed or deep-dish. My apologies to the city of Chicago!
- **Cheese**
  Not all cheeses are created equal. There is a spectrum, so choose wisely.
  Soft cheeses naturally tend to have less fat than hard cheeses. Use organic when possible, like cheddar, feta, parmesan, and of course, mozzarella! Mozzarella has the least calories of the bunch, offering seventy calories per ounce, five grams of protein, and five grams of fat.
  Bad choices are anything processed or labeled "low-fat."
- **Toppings**
  Oh my goodness, toppings alone could be an entire book, so I won't bore you. To sum it up, use single-ingredient foods, which are foods that come directly from Mother Earth, no FDA nutritional label required.
  Good choices include pineapple, peppers, spinach, garlic, onions, mushrooms, basil, artichoke, tomatoes, broccoli, an over-easy egg, and grilled chicken.

Bad choices include super salty or processed foods that come with labels: bacon, prosciutto, sausage, pepperoni ... you get the idea.

I know what you're thinking, *Duh! You're not telling me anything I don't already know.* The truth is I'm just slapping you in the face with it. I'm giving you permission to eat the right *kind* of pizza, guilt-free, and to enjoy it with your beloved family and friends.

Now if only feeding my kid was this easy.

Create a Healthy Habit Pizza for Kids

This section is for anyone with a picky eater at home. If that's not you, then skip ahead to chapter 2. Because pizza is so loved by children everywhere, I taught a family fitness class where we crafted our own paper version of a Healthy Habit Pizza puzzle. The kids got to make it themselves and take it home to keep as a friendly reminder. The first five slices represent a different dietary habit, but the last three are just as important for food consumption to do its job.

healthy habit pizza

1 DRINK WATER
Half your body weight
in ounces

2 EAT FRUITS
Nature's candy, yummy!

3 EAT VEGGIES
Preferably the green ones

4 EAT CARBS & PROTEINS
At every meal

5 TAKE YOUR VITAMINS
Ask your doc for
recommendations

6 PRACTICE GOOD HYGIENE
Brush teeth, wash hands, shower

7 BE ACTIVE
30+ minutes of elevated
heart rate

8 GET SOME SLEEP
9+ hours for growing kids
7+ hours for adults

The kids get to decorate the paper slices with the appropriate buzz words, fun drawings, cute stickers, or relevant magazine pictures, while learning about why each one is an important and necessary part of living a healthy lifestyle. All the pizza slices are to be removed daily, and they have to earn each piece back by completing it in real life. Come bedtime, they should have completed the entire pizza pie, earning themselves a sticker!

All of us need accountability, but kids especially need visuals, charts, small rewards, and so on, until it eventually becomes a habit. It's kind of like putting on your seat belt when you get into the car. No one has to tell you to do it; your brain just works on autopilot and does it on its own. But it wasn't always that way. An adult once had to constantly remind you to "buckle up," and then it eventually became second nature. This Healthy Habit Pizza can be used as a tool for elementary-age kids to create their own healthy eating habits.

To try this DIY project at home, you will need the following:

- two thick paper plates (one to cut, and one that stays whole)
- markers, pictures, or stickers to decorate each slice with
- eight Velcro stickers to make the puzzle pieces stay in place

"Food is our common ground, a universal experience."
-James Beard

Since we can't just hit the delete button on the life tasks of buying food, occasionally preparing a meal or two, snacking, dining out, enjoying desserts, or socializing, we might as well make it a team effort and hold one another accountable. It takes a village to figure this out, and it's a constantly evolving journey. Think of all the fad diets and juice cleanses as your own weight-management seesaw ride, but the person on the other end of the seesaw is you! Freshman fifteen, up. Wedding dress goal, down. Baby weight, up. Beach vacation, down. Thanksgiving to New Years, up. Read a motivating book, down. Suffered a loss, up.

Yes, it will happen. You can burn fat, and you can build muscle, but they are two separate elements inside your body. You can't turn fat into muscle. And unfortunately, you can't out-exercise bad nutrition. Believe me ... I've tried.

Books to help defuse the stubborn food bomb!

The Virgin Diet by J.J. Virgin: In this book, she promises to show you how to lose seven pounds in just seven days, by dropping seven food groups from your diet. This requires some serious discipline, however, because you must eliminate all gluten, dairy, eggs, soy, corn, peanuts, and all forms of sugar from your diet. Since I didn't have seven pounds to lose, I read it strictly out of curiosity and to have on hand to help any clients that I thought might find her information useful. Don't worry though; you do get to add each of the food groups back into your diet, one by one. The concept is smart, and widely practiced by doctors who have to create a baseline for their patients with unexplainable digestion issues, intense migraines, unwarranted fatigue, or frequent body aches and pains. If that sounds like you, it couldn't hurt to give it a try!

The Virgin Diet Cookbook by J.J. Virgin, was written as a follow up to help you better navigate through your own food intolerances.

Making The Cut by Jillian Michaels: I know what you're thinking, and no, I'm not biased because of her name, I really do like her! Not that we've actually met, but I feel like we'd probably be friends. In this book, she promises to show you how to drop the last stubborn ten to twenty pounds once and for all. You just need to follow these seven rules for the next thirty days: 1. Know what your calorie intake should be and stick to it 2. Eat for your metabolic type 3. Eat ever four hours 4. No processed or junk foods 5. Consume less sodium and more water 6. No booze 7. Keep a food journal. A quick test will reveal if you are considered to be a slow, balanced, or fast oxidizer. Breakfast, lunch, snack, and dinner menus are provided for each oxidizer type. She then demonstrates a plethora of workouts to do at home or at the gym.

Master Your Metabolism by Jillian Michaels, was written two years later, and is a no-nonsense look at understanding your hormones and the roles they play inside of your body, especially in reaction to what you are feeding it. You will then have the knowledge to remove antinutrients, restore power nutrients, and lastly, rebalance with enough sleep and proper exercise for maximum metabolic impact. There are straightforward meal plans, recipes and shopping lists for up to fourteen days.

book club

DISCUSSION QUESTIONS

What's your favorite beverage that you enjoy only as a special treat?

_____

_____

> "Keep it neat or on the rocks, and alternate alcoholic drinks with a glass of water!"
> —Sara Shaughnessy (marketer for a liquor distributor)

What is your favorite healthy recipe to make at home?

_____

_____

What is your favorite restaurant to go to that has healthy options on the menu?

_____

_____

chapter 2

FITNESS BOMB

understanding the human body (and the way it works) is certainly no exception. I don't want a trainer to simply tell me to breathe, stand up tall, or engage my core. I want to know *why* I need to inhale when you say so, and what will happen to me if I don't. And why is maintaining a "neutral spine" so damn important anyway?

Think about your top five basic activities in a typical day and how each one of them is usually done while seated with the shoulders rounding forward. Some of the most common basic activities are as follows:

- sleeping in fetal position
- eating (at least three times a day)
- driving or riding in a car
- operating a computer
- using the restroom

Maybe you watch TV, read a book, sit in a classroom, or work in an office while seated for long stretches of time. You get where I'm going with this. How can we possibly be expected to have good posture when the majority of our waking (and sleeping) hours are practically prohibiting us from doing so?

The answer is simple: muscle memory. When you are working out (no matter what type of exercise you have chosen to do), do not, I repeat, *do not* think about anything besides doing that particular movement. We all know that being in the present moment is important. But not just for those special life moments, such as when you're saying your wedding vows or seeing your newborn baby for the first time. It is critical for your physical safety to be aware of what is initiating a movement in your body. Let me ask you this. Can you live without arms? The answer is yes, yes you can. It would be inconvenient and make life more challenging, but it can be done. But can you live without the trunk of your body? The "powerhouse" (as we call it in Pilates) is your core; it houses your digestive organs, liver, kidney, lungs, and heart. The answer is no, no you cannot. Why do you think police officers wear bulletproof vests? So please start focusing on engaging the part of your body that you cannot live without.

The Spine is the Lifeline of the Body

To fully understand the benefits of good posture, let's first learn what actually makes up the spine. It consists of many vertebrae, each one with a spongy material (nucleus pulposus) in between them. Starting at the top, you have seven cervical vertebrae (located behind the neck), twelve thoracic vertebrae (making up the majority of the back), five lumbar vertebrae (found in the lower back), then lastly, the large, triangular sacral bone and coccyx (the tailbone). When in proper alignment, the spine is the body's natural shock absorber. "When you move from poor posture to good posture, you increase levels of 'go-go-go' hormones, such as dopamine, as well as feel-good serotonin, plus you decrease the stress hormone cortisol," says Kenneth Hansraj, MD, a spinal surgeon in New York City. Neutral spine also helps to alleviate pressure from excess weight or sudden impact, such as a car accident, falling down, or even from doing a strenuous workout while in poor form. Well, for that last one, not on my watch!

good posture : bad posture

STANDING

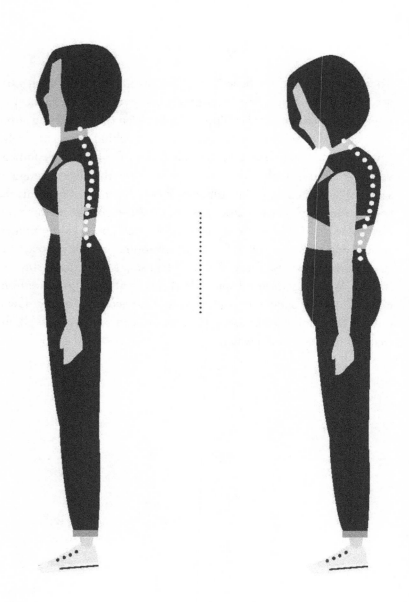

Dots are for representational purposes only. Not actual vertebrae.

good posture : bad posture

TEXTING

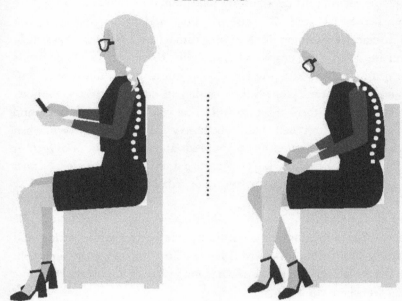

SITTING AT THE COMPUTER

Dots are for representational purposes only. Not actual vertebrae.

When you constantly slouch, many negative things will begin to happen inside of your body. Your spine is no longer in neutral alignment, and you are now entering the poor-posture zone (dun, dun, duuun). This type of hunched-over posture will squish your lungs and diaphragm, causing less air to enter them, almost like breathing through a straw. When you slouch, you are also compressing your colon, similar to stepping on a hose that is turned on and expecting water to come out easily, it's unrealistic. Your internal organs can't properly do what they are designed to do, so the body improvises. Shortness of breath will make you more easily fatigued and thus constantly feel tired. Think about how you instinctually yawn when you're tired. It's because your brain needs an espresso shot of oxygen! A compressed colon will make you constipated and therefore bloated. Neither one is something I want to experience on a daily basis. Do you?

If not, have someone you trust take three pictures of you from a side view—one while standing naturally, one of you while sitting and texting, and another while working at your computer. Compare them to the pictures shown above of what good versus bad posture looks like and see where you fit in.

The first short-term fix to improving your posture is just being aware and then constantly adjusting the way you sit throughout the day. You can't fix something you didn't even know was incorrect to begin with. Second is doing a chest-opener stretch many times throughout the day. Lie down, placing a pool noodle, long bolster, or foam roller down the center of your back, and place your hands in cactus pose (some call it goal post) where your arms are out to the side at a ninety degree angle. This lifts your torso off the ground enough to force a deep stretch in the pectoralis minor (the armpits) and the pectoralis major (behind the breast tissue). These muscles are not used to being pulled in this direction, so it will be uncomfortable. You could also feel your chest open by standing in a doorway while in cactus pose with your forearms against the doorframe; keeping your hips square, and stepping forward through the door.

Let's revisit the top five basic activities in a typical day and make some tweaks.

- Try to sleep on your back with a pillow under your knees to create neutral spine.
- Eat meals slower, being aware of resetting your shoulders back and down.
- Adjust the seat and mirrors in your car so they make you sit up nice and tall.
- Convert to using a rising desk that allows you to stand up at your computer.
- Don't use your Smartphone while in the restroom. Get done and get out!

Correcting bad posture long term is accomplished by developing a stronger core.

"No matter the question, the answer is always core."
-Shana Mayerson

Let's just say you are doing a basic bicep curl with a ten-pound weight in your hand. Close your eyes and do this motion in your head. Where is the movement coming from? If you're at the gym and thinking about what you're going to make for dinner, or the massive pile of laundry you still haven't put away, then the movement is probably coming from your hand. Fun fact: whatever initiates a movement is reaping the majority of the benefit of that exercise. So why exactly is the hand starting the movement in a bicep curl? Well, it shouldn't be. Now focus on your breath instead of the ten-pound weight in your hand. Breathing is literally the very first thing we all do in our entire lives, and thus we tend to take it for granted. So let's fix this, shall we?

Every Movement Has an Extension and a Flexion

The extension is going to be easier. That's when you take a deep inhale, filling your lungs and diaphragm with delicious oxygen. In this example, it's when you lower the forearm down toward the earth's natural gravitational pull. You can also think of cow pose in yoga. The spine drops down, the eyes look up, and you breathe in.

The flexion is going to be harder. That's when you make an intentional exhale, forcing the breath to allow your blood to flow throughout the body and help you achieve the more challenging part of the exercise. In this example, it's curling the forearm with the weight upward against gravity. You can also think of cat pose in yoga. When the spine curves up, it's an abdominal crunch, the eyes look to the belly button, and you exhale.

Think about where the exhale is taking place. Is it coming from your hand? Nope, it's coming from your trunk! That's where your lungs are and where your heart is beating, sending oxygen and blood to the large and small muscles, then lastly toward the hand holding the ten-pound weight. So your thoughts should not be focusing on the extremities but rather your core. The extremities will eventually get the message. I promise.

Think of your pelvic floor as the very first domino in a long, bendy line, and your fingers (or toes) as representing the last ten dominoes. Once the first domino falls, it sends the message to the next one to fall over, etcetera, etcetera. Eventually, ta-da, they're all down! That's how your exercise movements should be done as well, but instead of falling, it's engaging.

I'm often asked how to engage a muscle. At first, I was shocked that people didn't know this. But I have since learned that there's no silly question, and if one person is wondering it, others might be as well. To engage a muscle is simply to give it an internal squeeze. I can almost guarantee that you do this on a daily basis without even knowing it. For instance, here are some examples:

Q: If you saw that you were about to get rammed in the stomach by (let's just say) a forty-pound child running straight toward you at full speed ahead, what would you do?

A: Quickly firm up your abs by giving them an internal squeeze, to lessen pain from the impact.

Q: If you're hanging out by the pool in a swimsuit and your friend opens up her phone to snap a #sundayfunday picture for her Instagram followers, what would you do? (Besides throwing her phone into the pool.)

A: Quickly firm up your abs by giving them an internal squeeze, so your abs look more defined.

Q: If you're two vodka tonics in at a concert and you suddenly have to pee *so* badly, but realize there are about twenty drunk people ahead of you in line, what would you do?

A: Quickly engage your Kegel muscles by giving them an internal squeeze, so you don't pee your pants!

Imagine you are sitting in a circle with your friends playing the game telephone—a classic and favorite camp game of mine. The first person (the powerhouse) gets to make up a silly sentence. She then whispers it to the next person (the connecting muscle) and so on and so forth. The sentence will eventually reach the last person (the extremity) in the circle, but it has to go through everyone else first—just like your exercise movements need to start at the core and then travel all the way to the end of your (less important) limbs. Now, are you still going to tell me you don't know how to engage a muscle? Of course you do! Notice how the engaging is always coming from the core parts of the body, never the extremities.

Now Back to Muscle Memory

If you are breathing correctly when you're working out, meaning with intention and from (you guessed it) the core, then it will soon feel more natural to also breathe correctly when you're eating, driving, working, and so on. Because in order to breathe 100 percent correctly, you anatomically cannot be slouched or hunched over. You just can't.

Another question I get asked quite often is about flexibility. I'm nearing forty and can do the splits. I haven't always been able to do the splits. I decided as an adult that I was going to make it a personal goal of mine. There is a secret to accomplishing this, and I'm going to share it with you right now. Are you ready for it? Do you need to grab a highlighter? This is top secret information, people. Here it is ...

Drink lots of water and stretch daily.

Yup, every single day of the week that ends in y. What, you were hoping for something easier? Sorry, not sorry! I can't tell you the amount of clients I've had over the years who say they want to be more flexible, but the only time they stretch is when they're with me. Seriously? It's literally like going to the dentist and complaining that you have cavities. But then when the dental hygienist asks how often you brush your teeth, you answer with a straight face, "About twice a week." Obviously you'll have cavities if you brush only twice a week! Just like obviously your muscles are going to be tight if you stretch only twice a week. You drink and eat food every single solitary day. Just like you move your bones and muscles in some way, shape, or form every single day. You wouldn't brush your teeth only on days that you eat cake, so don't only stretch your body on days that you work out!

As for water consumption, if you're dehydrated, your body will preserve any water it gets for the most important things first, like hydrating your blood, not your muscles. Think of your muscles like a sponge. When a sponge is wet, it's more pliable. When it is dry, it shrinks and becomes stiff. For the sake of easy math, if you weigh one hundred pounds, you divide that number in half to get fifty. That's how many ounces of water you would need to drink each day to stay well hydrated. So please, for the love of God, don't complain about being inflexible when you're drinking Diet Coke every day (gag) and only stretching after workouts. It's like trying to win the lottery but never actually buying a ticket. It's just not going to happen.

What Goes Around Comes Around

Imagine walking into a daycare facility filled with a bunch of one-year-olds first learning how to walk. They're wobbly, unsure of what each step will provide, holding onto anything and everything within reach. Their core is underdeveloped, naturally, and the world's surfaces seem uncertain. Now picture yourself walking into a nursing home. The aging senior citizens are wobbly, unsure of what each step will provide, holding onto anything and everything within reach. Their core is underdeveloped, due to lack of use, and the world's surfaces seem scary.

As you age, your balance will start to go. It's a fact of life, and it has to do with our inner ear canal and the tiny little hairs within it, blah blah blah. Ask an ENT about this; it's quite fascinating. However, since we can't prevent that from happening, we might as well attempt to maintain what we *can* control. It has been proven time and again that with better balance, a stronger core, and more flexibility, you are less likely to trip and fall and severely injure yourself. The trifecta is as follows:

- balance
- strength
- flexibility

Sorry, pharmaceutical companies, but prevention truly is the absolute best medicine! For good overall health, which will ease you into getting older more gracefully, you need to include a combination of maintaining good balance, gaining lean muscle mass, and improving flexibility. Because guess what? If you don't use it, you lose it. That's right. I said it. Our bodies are smart, and they are designed to adapt to our needs. Have you ever watched a bunch of seven-year-old kids playing at recess without a care in the world? Skinning their knees, hair is a mess, just climbing, skipping, and running like the wind. Sadly, as they become older and more self-conscious of what other kids think of them, they no longer act as carefree. Their heart adapts, and their metabolism slows down. The next time they attempt to "run like the wind," they just might feel like the wind is being knocked out of them instead. As an adult, how you feel after the first run of ski season (horrible) compared to the last run of ski season (unstoppable) is going to be drastically noticeable. The same concept applies here but in reverse. If you *do* use it, you *don't* lose it!

What happens to a perfectly good car if you don't drive it for five years? The oil doesn't get changed, the old gas just sits there, the leather starts to crack, the metal gets rusty, and so on. Now take that identical car but drive it around town for five years, performing regular maintenance requirements, giving it the occasional car wash, and so on. Which one is going to be more reliable to you when you need it? I don't know about you, but I'll take the one with more miles on it that has been well maintained. Now apply that same concept to your body. Yes, you can jump-start the car or take it to a pricey repair shop. Just like you can wake up one day and decide to start working out, make better food choices, or schedule a pricey elective surgery. If that's you, that's awesome that you finally woke up! But if you've never experienced a health rut before, then hopefully my car analogy will remind you to stay on the prevention route.

Don't Hate Being Sore

If you understood why you were sore, then you might not hate it so much. When you challenge a muscle past its comfort level, you are creating tiny little tears in it that need to be repaired. That sounds worse than it is. Those tears now have two possible outcomes. (1) they can close right back up, and you're starting over from square one the next time you work out, or (2) they can fill in with new muscle fibers, and then the muscle becomes stronger!

If you don't exercise regularly, drink enough water daily, consume plenty of protein-rich foods, or stretch the muscles you fatigued, then the tiny tears will close back up rather quickly. If you continue to work out a few times a week, drink half your body weight (in ounces) of water, consume plenty of amino acids, and hold challenging stretches, your muscle will then begin to grow while you're sleeping and your body is at rest. So yes, sleep is important!

Stretching Is Not Boring

Have you ever watched a baby just naturally wake up from his or her nap? No alarm clock to jolt him up and out of bed, no awareness of time or day. Their eyes slowly scan the room, and then it happens ... the most delicious, deep, animalistic stretch of the baby's limbs! The back becomes arched, elbows are locked and reaching for the neighbor's house, and the legs have a mind of their own. Then after a moment of calm and another blink of the eyes, realization of a very wet diaper and being extremely parched sets in. But none of that came about until after the daily instinctual stretch of the body as if it were Gumby himself. Why does this natural instinct go away? It's not like on your fifth birthday someone whispers to you, "Okay, it's time to stop stretching in the mornings now." But somehow it slowly vanishes from our routine. Instead, our minds are now playing a constant game of chess from the moment the alarm goes off or the lights go on. We're thinking two, maybe three moves ahead of the move we're currently in. Is it going to rain today? Did I take out the trash last night? Is the milk in the fridge expired? The list goes on, and notice there's no mention of a single stretch. Our animal instincts are lost, because we now have awareness of time, days, and our life's many obligations and responsibilities.

Someone once told me that every morning you get the chance to plant a seed and watch it grow. The first thing you give attention to when you wake up is the metaphorical seed that you're planting for the rest of your day. If you're someone who gets FOMO (fear of missing out) when you look at your friends' social media posts, or gets anxiety when looking at the mountain of emails in your inbox, or even depressed from watching the morning news, then don't let those be the first things you see in the morning. Your thoughts are literally dictating your mood for the rest of the day. Do you want to grow something sour or sweet? If the answer is sweet, try to wake up more slowly. Put a big smile on your face, and it will trick the brain into thinking that you are happy (first seed planted; positivity). Stretch your limbs like a cat basking in the sunlight of an East facing window (second seed planted; agility). Grab a crystal or stone from a bowl near your bed and keep it on you the rest of the day. They are smooth to the touch, beautiful to the eye, and natural gifts from the earth (third seed planted; reminding you to stay strong, grounded, and centered).

And You're Off!

Hungry but in a hurry? Good thing you have a cornucopia of drive-through windows and Uber Eats, Grubhub, Postmates, DoorDash, and Bite Squad to rely on. When you need to get in a workout but are in a hurry, what do you do? Well, now you can do my fitness-on-the-go tips. It's something I do on a daily basis, and is super easy. You just sneak in tiny little bite size exercises throughout the day, anytime you're forced to sit or stand in one place for an extended period of time. Bonus, it also helps to pass the time more quickly. So try these out the next time you find yourself in one of the following scenarios:

- **Brushing your teeth, or using mouthwash**
  You could hover over your sink like the Hunchback of Notre Dame, foaming at the mouth, or you could hold a wall-sit and work the quadriceps, which are found in the upper thighs. Your knees are to be bent like you're sitting in an invisible chair, and your back is flat against the wall. Electronic toothbrushes usually have a two-minute timer on them, which is a challenging yet doable amount of time to hold a wall-sit. Your thighbone, known as the femur, is the longest and strongest bone in the body.

- **Waiting in line to check out**
  The grocery store, pharmacy, post office, dry cleaners, bathroom line, Target checkout—you can't tell me a single day passes where you don't have to wait in at least one line. What I do in this situation is calf raises! Slowly raising and lowering your heels requires no more space than you're already taking up anyway. It challenges your balance and works the calves, ankles, Achilles' heel, gastrocnemius, and arch support, all at once! No need to count reps, because you're doing both feet at the same time. Yes, the person behind you might notice, but

honestly, no one has ever called me out on it before, unless maybe to compliment me on my defined calf muscles!

- **Waiting at a red light in the car**
  I use this opportunity to reset my posture. Roll the shoulders back and down, opening up the chest. Sit up nice and tall and then adjust the rearview mirror if it needs it, which it likely will. Then take a few deep breaths if time permits. Always inhale through the nose, then slowly and deliberately exhale through either the nose (yoga practice) or the mouth (Pilates practice), as long as it's coming from the back of the throat, not the belly. Repeat until the light turns green. I think it goes without saying to always keep your eyes open.

- **Watching the microwave timer count backward**
  Don't just stand there staring at the numbers decreasing like it's December 31 and you're waiting for Anderson Cooper and Andy Cohen to yell, "Happy New Year!" Instead, you could throw your foot up on a nearby counter or back of a sofa and hold a hamstring stretch until the beep goes off. Make sure both legs are straight, the spine is long, and the hips are square. Because the microwave is already timing you, just divide that number in half so you know when to switch legs. You could also hold a figure-four stretch (also known as a standing pigeon) to get the piriformis muscle in the glute, hip, and outer thigh. That's when the standing leg is straight, but the lower half of the stretching leg is resting on the counter or back of a sofa, spine is long, and hips are square.

- **Putting away the laundry**
  Full disclosure, this process is not a shortcut to doing laundry, but it does allow you to get in more steps, which is especially good if you're wearing a smartwatch device that holds you accountable for your movement. Have the clothes already folded and the hangers ready to go in the laundry room. Hang up two items, speed walk them to the appropriate closet, then come back and do it again with two more items until the laundry is all put away. I know, this

is not a time saver per se, but it's a great way to get your heart rate up while doing a tedious task that has to be done anyway. This is an even better workout if your laundry room is on a different floor from your closets. Yay! No need to arrange childcare, no monthly membership fees, and you can even multitask by simultaneously listening to your favorite podcast or audio book. It's a win-win!

- **Waiting in a parked car to pick someone up**
  If you feel like you're in a safe place and the weather permits it, get out and take a brisk walk until the person is ready to go. You will be squeezing in lots of extra steps on a day that you may have thought you didn't have time for a workout at all.

Post yourself completing one (or more) of my fitness-on-the-go tips to Instagram and tag me @the_5_f_bombs to help motivate other readers and to show that it can be done!

On Your Mark, Get Set, Go!

The problem I've noticed with getting people to *start* to exercise is that they think it's an all-or-nothing commitment. "If I can't commit to a full hour, at least three days a week, then I might as well do nothing at all." Well that's a bunch a bologna. It's like saying, "If I can't commit to making a four-course dinner from scratch, then we're just not eating dinner at all." Lies! You can still heat up something from the freezer, order a pizza, eat leftovers, or make breakfast for dinner; you don't just skip dinner. So if you're already sneaking in my fitness-on-the-go tips, then hitting the gym maybe once a week, or streaming a YouTube video from your living room after everyone else in the house has fallen asleep, then guess what? You did it! You had the exercise equivalent of emergency freezer food for dinner, because something is always better than nothing. You wouldn't go to bed hungry, so don't go to bed without knowing that you've challenged your body in some small way.

The key to making or setting goals is to be realistic. Let's start by comparing it to building a house. Not that I have the training of an actual architect (because I don't) but I do have years of hands-on experience of being a playful child, a teenage babysitter, and a mom in her thirties. These various life stages allowed me the opportunity to play with wooden blocks, LEGO bricks, and create many professional-grade pillow forts, if I do say so myself. From that, my common sense has taught me that you don't start with the roof! It's true, you just wouldn't, that would be ridiculous! So why then do women set goals of wearing a size 4? That's equivalent to the "roof" in this scenario; it's the final step in the process. It's no wonder so many of us can't reach our goals. We haven't yet laid the proper foundation, ran wires for electrical, installed access to plumbing, or even built sturdy walls. We went straight to the roofing store to pick out the shingles and thought, "fuck, I can't buy these, life sucks." The point is, create smaller to-do lists along the way and then constantly cross them off and add new ones on until eventually the end goal is realistic and in sight. This makes hitting all of life's little accomplishments along the way, that much more rewarding too. Stop reading right now, put a bookmark in this page, and make a list of attainable goals... Go!

"What's the best type of workout to do?"
-Every client I've ever trained

I get asked this question all the time, and unfortunately, there's not one "best" type of workout. It's about finding the one that works best for *you*! So with all of those options out there, you'd think that surely you can find "the one" that matches with your physical capabilities, hours of operation, proximity to home, and fits within your budget. First answer these questions and then get your butt moving!

exercise flow chart

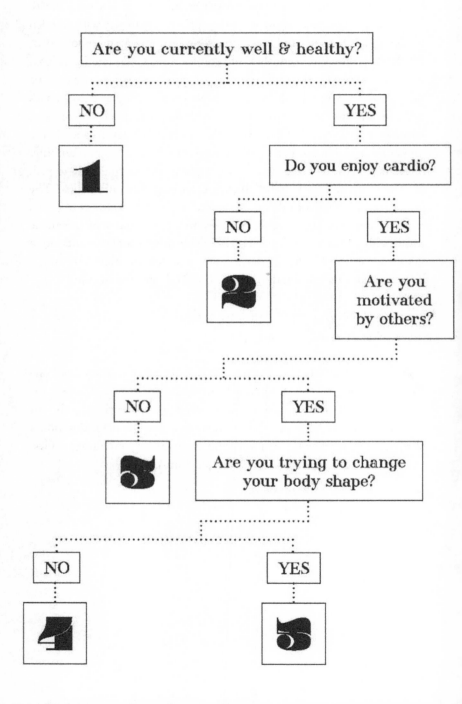

Are you currently well & healthy?

- NO → **1**
- YES → **Do you enjoy cardio?**
  - NO → **2**
  - YES → **Are you motivated by others?**
    - NO → **3**
    - YES → **Are you trying to change your body shape?**
      - NO → **4**
      - YES → **5**

exercise answers

Please consult your doctor for physical activity advice if you're recovering from an injury or surgery, or are currently pregnant.

Try Yoga, Pilates, Barre, Tai Chi, long walks holding light weights, or water aerobics.

Liar, liar, pants on fire. You may not even realize it, but when your best friend works her butt off and loses 10 pounds, she is subconsciously motivating you. The people you choose to follow on social media are secretly inspiring you to want to be the best version of yourself.

Congratulations, you're a unicorn!

A realtor would say, the three most important things about buying a house are *"location, location, location"*. Well as a trainer, I would say the three most important things about a workout plan are *"accountability, accountability, accountability"*. So find yourself a workout partner or hire a trainer, and try out every single exercise there is until you find what excites you. I mean, really tickles your fancy! Try Zumba, Spin, CrossFit, TRX, boxing, or HIIT Circuit Training classes. Maybe even invest in a smart watch (Apple, Fitbit, or Polar) to help hold you accountable for your daily movement.

But, what's that you say? You don't have time? When people say, "I don't have time to work out," what they're really saying is, "It's not a priority for me right now." So the next time someone invites you to start a fitness regimen, try saying *that* instead. You will feel ridiculous, as you should. Because as Joseph Pilates once said, "Physical fitness is the first requisite of happiness," and he's not wrong, and you know it. He was just ahead of his time, that's all. After completing a really challenging workout in the morning, the rest of the day will seem like a cakewalk. Need to finish that report for your boss? Easy-peasy compared to the twenty burpees you did earlier in less than three minutes! It's probably similar to how Spiderman must have felt after he got bit by the spider. Unstoppable! Being physically active can provide a better, more natural mental boost than even a cup of coffee, and it has longer-lasting benefits, especially if inversions are involved. Allowing your body to be inverted, putting the head below the heart, either while in down dog, a headstand, or even just hinging forward to hold a stretch while reaching for the ground, sends a surge of oxygen to the brain, providing benefits similar to a big, fat, delicious yawn! Now, thanks to your morning workout, you really can be more productive in a shorter amount of time.

Squats, Sit-Ups & Push-Ups

The three most common exercises that women often do slightly incorrectly are squats, sit-ups, and push-ups. This is simply due to a lack of proprioception, or our awareness of body alignment. Making a few simple changes in your form will actually make an enormous difference in both the safety and effectiveness of the exercises themselves.

- **Squats**
  The next time you squat, try doing them with your toes lifted off the ground. This will ensure your weight is shifted back into the heels, removing any excess pressure from the knees. When you squat with your feet parallel to each other, you're activating the front of the thighs. But when you squat with

your feet turned out, you're activating the inner thighs, and most women need stronger adductors but already have pretty strong quads.

- **Sit-Ups**
Instead of allowing your fingers to "weave a basket" behind your head, place "spirit fingers" (also known as jazz hands) behind your ears. This will allow the head to follow the lead of the abs instead of initiate the crunch movement. Pick a spot to focus on that is roughly about where the ceiling meets the wall. This will keep the chin away from the chest, allowing your neck to remain in neutral alignment, preventing neck pain.

- **Push-Ups**
Women all too often say that they can't do push-ups. They then modify by lowering to their knees. To me, that is not a modification; it's an entirely different exercise and will not help you build the strength you need to do regular push-ups. Instead, hold a perfect form plank. The booty should be in line between the ankles and shoulders, the neck is long, and shoulders are stacked directly over the wrists. Once you can hold this for thirty seconds, add one push-up. Each day, do it again and try adding on another push-up. If you want to modify, think of a tripod. The farther apart your hands are from each other, the easier the plank or push-up will be. The reverse is true as well. If your feet are touching each other, the weight distribution changes, and this tripod becomes more like a table with four legs, which is much more stable. Also make sure that the veins inside your arms are facing forward, not inward, in order to activate the triceps more than the shoulders.

"If you want something you've never had, you must be willing to do something you've never done."
-Thomas Jefferson

- having good posture
- developing a strong core
- staying well hydrated
- daily stretching
- consistent workouts

"All progress takes place outside the comfort zone."
-Michael John Bobak

Now that you've committed to this new workout plan, are you going to stick with it? If you can really grasp the *why* part of fitness, then I think you will. Let's just say that you finally splurged and spent thousands of dollars on that designer handbag you've been drooling over for god-knows-how-long. How would you treat it? Would you toss a bunch of sticky junk into it? Let it get all dirty, broken, or misshapen? Of course not! So why would you treat your body that way? I'm certain that your self-worth is valued at a higher price tag than a designer handbag. Understanding the importance of defusing the fitness bomb is one thing. However, actually putting it into practice on a daily basis should ultimately culminate in living a longer, healthier, and more active lifestyle. Without all of the pieces working together, your fitness success will be something you constantly struggle with. Life-changing healthy habits start now.

Make healthier food choices
+ Move your body more often
= Weight loss and stronger body

It's just that simple!

book club

DISCUSSION QUESTIONS

What is one thing you took away from this chapter that you didn't already know?

_____

_____

What are your personal health or fitness goals for the year, and what are your plans to reach them?

_____

_____

If you could do only three exercises for the rest of your life, what would they be?

_____

_____

"Deadlifts, squats, and rows."
—Courtney Bentley (personal trainer and founder of the *Fit Fierce and Fabulous* podcast)

"Squat plus overhead press with a kettlebell, burpees, and ball slams."
—Monica Daggs (fitness model, personal trainer, and PowerHour360 gym manager)

chapter 3

FRIEND BOMB

"I'll be there for you, cause you're there for me too."

-The Rembrandts

Friends are the family that we ultimately choose ourselves. They're the ones who we enjoy the fun holidays with, like Superbowl Sunday, Fourth of July, and Halloween. We share in their countless wedding festivities, such as engagement parties, bridal showers, bachelorette parties, rehearsal dinners, evening receptions, and farewell brunches. We celebrate every milestone, both good and bad, together. We all want female friendships, gal pals, soul sisters, whatever term you want to use. It fills an emotional need in us that our loving spouses and adorable children just can't meet, and that's okay. If you're lucky, a true friend will lend you anything from a party dress to a bed to sleep in, an unbiased opinion, or maybe even an organ.

Family Friends Are the Best of Friends

My grandparents, Evie and Al, had two other couples who they did everything with. The six of them took vacations together every year, celebrated all the holidays together, even had babies at the same time (my mom being one of those babies), and those kids were like family to one another. So much so, that by the time I came along, a product of the third generation, I thought we really were cousins! It wasn't until I was in high school and questioned the connection to my "cousin" Ilana. My mom laughed and explained that she wasn't my cousin at all, just close family friends. All that time, and I had no idea. I was shocked! All of those "family members" have been at every wedding, bar mitzvah, and funeral that my family has ever had. They've added love and joy to any happy occasion and have helped ease the pain and sorrow from sad ones. It just goes to show that real friendships are like rainbows; you don't get to enjoy the colorful beauty without also enduring the wet rain. Family means commitment to one another, not necessarily just sharing a bloodline.

Hi, Neighbor

One morning, there happened to be a magnificent owl perched on the roof of the vacant house that sits directly between me and our new neighbors, whom we hadn't met yet. My son and I stared at the stillness of this majestic creature, and I knew his beauty had to be shared before he flew away, never to be seen again. It's common knowledge that owls are nocturnal creatures and definitely shouldn't be sunbathing on rooftops in the middle of summer in Las Vegas. That's when I decided that we should meet our new neighbors. My son and I rang their doorbell just two short weeks after I saw the moving truck unloading a family's entire life's belongings into their new home. I figured that was long enough to get settled in, right? We were instantly greeted with a welcoming smile and an excited "Hi!" as if we were old friends. Our kids adore each other, our husbands are man-besties, we take an annual family ski trip together, and the rest is history! If you don't at least try to meet new people, they will always remain strangers, no matter what. If you don't ask for what you want, the answer is always going to be no.

Social Wellness

Having a social life outside of your family life is just plain good for the soul. These people are spending time with you because they *want* to, not because they have a DNA obligation. And that makes us feel good inside. A recent survey by AARP found that one in three adults (forty-five and older) suffers from loneliness, which carries the same amount of health risks as smoking fifteen cigarettes a day. It's shocking, I know! But how do female adults make new girlfriends if they move to a new city or all their friends have moved away? It can be a difficult task if you don't have kids or don't work with people who you would want to hang out with, but it is possible.

Try these out for starters:

- Do a quick online search for your college or sorority alumni group and then join. There's sometimes a small annual fee to be an active member but not always.
- Meet your neighbors. I know what you're thinking: *who knows their neighbors anymore?* But try it out. I dare you. Knock, knock! Who's there? "Hey, did you see this cool owl outside?" Or, "I was wondering who does your great landscaping, and could I get their information from you?"
- Join a local volunteer organization like the Junior League, an animal rescue shelter, or even a local food bank or homeless shelter. They are always looking for an extra set of helping hands. You will meet likeminded women and feed your soul at the same time.
- Join a women's group at your church or temple. If you're not a member of one yet, here's a good excuse to join. A lot of times, they offer Bunco nights, Mah-jongg, book clubs, bridge, lunch groups, and so on. It may take a few fails until you find a group of women you jive with, but once you do, it will have been well worth it.
- Join a small gym, go regularly, and before you know it, you will get to know the other regulars too. Then become social media friends, exchange numbers, or meet up afterward for coffee or smoothies. And, as a bonus, you'll be able to fit into your old jeans again!

You Already Have Your Girl-Gang Figured Out?

Good, because psychologists say they are able to predict how many friends a person has by how much pain they are able to withstand. And researchers have also found evidence that spending time with friends can increase production of oxytocin, the feel-good hormone. Dr. William Chopik, assistant professor of psychology at Michigan State University, found that adult friendships are a stronger predictor of good overall health and happiness versus having positive relationships with family members. Sorry, Mom. I still love you though! Maintaining those friendships becomes even more important as we grow older because we tend to get busier and have more responsibilities. It makes us feel validated to hang out with friends we can be ourselves with. In a 2017 study, the Mayo Clinic found that adults who play strategic board games together have a 22 percent lower risk of mild cognitive impairment. If you've ever watched someone you love suffer from Alzheimer's or dementia, then you have seen some of the horrific side effects of brain deterioration. So, while orchestrating a weekly game of chess with peers is by no means curing a disease, if it can prolong the onset and help maintain positive friendships at the same time, then sign me up!

Birds of a Feather

Your closest friends not only share your common interests but probably have a similar moral compass as you. They should never intentionally make you feel bad about yourself and provide emotional support or encouragement when needed. If you can check off those boxes, you've got yourself a keeper! It is often said that friends will come into your life for a reason, a season, or a lifetime. Each and every one has served a valuable purpose in some way or another. If a friend no longer brings you joy or has simply grown in a different direction, then it's probably time to let that friend go. Like the salad dressing in the back of the fridge, its expiration date has come and gone. People often say that ending a friendship feels equivalent to quitting a job or breaking up with a significant other, and I get that, but that doesn't mean it has to be messy. I've done the dramatic falling-out thing in my twenties, and it wasn't fun. My thirties have taught me that you *can* part ways while remaining on good terms. People do it all the time.

Namaste and Cabernet

Coordinate a small group of girls (at least 4 or more) and plan a weekend getaway somewhere fun! Picture a morning yoga class, relaxation, and an afternoon wine tour. Maybe even stay in a vacation rental home, so that you're all living together like pre-pubescent kids at sleep away camp! It's amazing how quickly bonds form when you're forced to live under one roof. Reality TV shows like *Big Brother*, *The Bachelor*, and *Real World*, is living proof of adults bonding in rapid time while cohabiting. Ideally, everyone is on an equal level of importance on the trip. Meaning it's not a bachelorette party or only one person's birthday. Set some clear guidelines about limited use of cell phones, not being negative, or anything that could ruin the positive vibe to which you're trying to create. If you are serious about improving your adult female friendships, make this trip a priority. Bonus, your family gets an opportunity to miss you and realize all that you do for them! And who knows, you might even end up missing your daily routine from home. Everyone will benefit from it in the end.

Not Everyone Hits the Jackpot—Quit While You're Ahead

I've lived in Las Vegas for fifteen years, and truth be told, I can probably count on my two hands the amount of times I have played a slot machine. Some people sit at those machines for hours on end, feeding their hard-earned cash into a shiny piece of metal that may or may not pay out in the end. The reason they can't walk away is likely because they need to "win big" in order to justify the money they've already invested into the machine. If they walk away at a loss, it's admitting defeat and time wasted that they'll never get back. I think that's why some women have a hard time letting go of friends who no longer serve them in a positive way. You may feel that all your time spent with them will have been for nothing, but I disagree. Happy memories are always a great treasure to have, and that friend once served a beautiful purpose in your life, even if it was for just a short while. Marie Kondo is known for asking people if certain items, like clothing or books, "spark joy," and if they don't, she suggests getting rid of it. Letting go of a toxic friendship (hopefully before a dramatic falling-out) is not an act of cruelty; it's simply an act of self-care. This is an example of the seesaw trying to balance at the pivot point.

When to Cut the Ties and Move On

When you see her name or picture pop up on your phone or social media feed, does it send a jolt of anxiety through your body? If so, her life stresses have become your life stresses, and that's not cool. She may be taking advantage of you and your kindness. Have any of your other friends or family members ever asked you why you're still friends with her? If so, you may be looking at her through tunnel vision, and they can see something in your periphery that you can't. Hindsight is always twenty-twenty. Before you even think about breaking up with a friend via text message or picking a fight, start by preoccupying your time that was previously spent on that person in a more productive way. Volunteering at school or starting a new part-time job are two great examples of constructive ways to spend your time and free up space for new friendships. Your physical and mental health are dependent upon distancing yourself from the people who you are not energetically aligned with. Chances are this friend was probably feeling the same way, and you just gave her the freedom to move on as well—all while keeping everything copacetic!

"A real friend is one who walks in when the rest of the world walks out."

–Walter Winchell

The next time you get invited to go out with old friends, new neighbors, or other families, simply say "yes." If you're asked to help volunteer for a good cause, put your lame excuses in the trash can and go do it. Part ways with the friends that start to feel like poison in your life and have fun on the metaphorical seesaw. As it turns out, it's good for your health. Years from now, you won't necessarily remember having a few extra bucks in your bank account or some extra minutes of sleep that night. But you will likely still have the memories you made from an awesome girls' night out with friends or accomplishing something that was for a greater good.

Books to help defuse the stubborn friend bomb!

Balanced and Beautiful by Katrina Scott and Karena Dawn: This five-day reset for your body, mind, and spirit, allows you to feel like you're actual besties with the Tone-It-Up beach babes themselves! These girls are as real as it gets and tell it like it is. They not only provide tips and tricks to refresh, motivate, inspire, energize, and relax, but they do it so that you can feel the smiles on their faces as you're reading each page! Colorful images, doable resipes,

Work Wife by Erica Cerulo and Clair Mazur: These successful, savvy, midwestern girls met in college and beat all odds of creating and sustaining a business that they were passionate about. That is true friendship! A book about fashionable, strong, entrepreneurial women who help inspire others, is a book I'm happy to recommend.

book club

DISCUSSION QUESTIONS

Do you know the people who live on your street, and would you be willing to ask them for a cup of sugar at a moments notice?

_____

_____

What are your personal social goals for the next year?

_____

_____

How did you meet your most recent new friends?

_____

_____

"When I move to a new city, I like to take an adult dance class, art class, sport, or any other activity. It's like social networking to get to know others."

—Danielle Stone (military wife)

chapter 4

FAMILY BOMB

Like a Thumbprint, No Two Families Are Exactly Alike

All families are unique in almost every possible way, which means no one can truly give advice on the topic at hand. There are so many variables and constantly moving parts it can be hard to even keep up. What I've observed from others and learned through my own experience is that being a mom, a wife, a daughter, or an aunt is no easy walk in the park for anyone. I don't care what their Instagram feed looks like. As a sophomore in college, I was introduced to the guy that my heart knew I wanted. We met at a Kappa Delta / AEPi mixer (that I planned, BTW) and exchanged numbers at the end of the night. I called him first because my friend Jane made me, but whatever. We went to dinner and a football game two days later and had a blast! The first time I went to his place and saw the horrible quadruple hand-me-down sofa taking residency in his frat house, I spontaneously said, "I can reupholster that, you know." His eyes immediately got wide and was mega impressed by this partial-lie. I say partial only because it may have been implied that I had, in fact, reupholstered a sofa before, which I technically hadn't. But it was also partially true because I was currently majoring in Fashion Design and Product Development and was the proud owner of a Viking sewing machine. Regardless of Truth v Lie it worked well as an excuse for him to call me again to get together. And sure enough, the following week we were strolling the isles of Jo-Ann's to buy fabric. Walking through his fraternity house carrying my sewing machine in one hand, and a caboodle full of notions in the other must have been quite a sight for the guys in the house. News spread fast and heads would occasionally pop in with requests like, "Hey, do you think you can sew up this hole in my jeans?" But guess what? That was 17 years ago and we're still together to this day! In life, if you don't at least ask or take a chance, then no matter what, that's where the story ends. Teetering somewhere in the unknown.

New Mamma Drama

Moms struggle to make life-altering decisions every single day. It starts before their child is even born. Deciding between a natural delivery, epidural, or C-section, then choosing the perfect name, breastmilk or formula, staying at home, dropping off at daycare, or hiring a nanny—the list goes on. As they grow, we are still in control of the dietary choices for these tiny, growing bodies and deciding what school will shape their little developing brains. We get the final say on sports, playdates, and transportation, all of which can and will alter their path in life, even in the smallest of ways. At what age do we allow them to get their first cell phone, start dating, drive a car, or work a real job? Ahhhh! There's just no black-and-white answer; everything falls under some sort of a gray. And when you're pregnant, you don't fully realize just how many unpaid jobs you have voluntarily signed yourself up for, no matter how many books you've read (this one included). Here's a small list of some work experience that, as a mom, you might be adding to your future résumé:

- **Event planner**
  Pinterest the crap out of a themed birthday party every year for your child and fifteen of their closest, snot-nosed friends.

- **Chef**
  Read chapter 1, "Food Bomb." Meal time again?

- **Secretary**
  Insert scheduling playdates, babysitters, and sports activities here.

- **Uber driver**
  I finally know my way around town, but sixteen still can't come soon enough.

- **Etiquette teacher**
  Did you remember to say "please" and "thank you?" Don't forget to wait your turn, share your toys, and keep your hands to yourself.

- **Twenty-four/seven Laundromat attendant**
  I chose to decorate the laundry room with fun colors, artwork, and happy pictures to make the room feel more inviting and the task seem less of a chore.

- **Amateur slinky detangler**
  Yup, it's a real skill; don't question it.

And many, many, many more …

A wellness special edition of *Time* magazine reported (in 2019) that only one in three kids is physically active in any vigorous way on a daily basis. This study horrified me and is the best way to show how important leading by example really is. A simple case of monkey see, monkey do. With increased weight comes a higher risk of type 2 diabetes, heart disease, and various cancers. Today's children are tomorrow's leaders of this world, whether we want to admit it or not. So, if they're bad leaders, is it going to be our fault? That's a lot of pressure to put on parents, grandparents, teachers, coaches, and so on, but it certainly is eye-opening. Any one person can say or do any one thing to a child that can either help or hinder them for the rest of their life. That's how powerful our actions are right now. Crazy! One thing's for sure. We will mess up. But we will also get some things right. We just have to hope that, in the end, the good times will outweigh the bad. This is when the seesaw is teeter tottering, balancing at the pivot point, and the new mamma drama has really set in.

Every Yin Needs a Yang

Unfortunately, I'm not a mind reader, and I haven't met anyone yet who actually is one. Since being passive-aggressive is a guaranteed recipe for marital disaster, the alternative is keeping an open dialogue. In a relaxed environment, occasionally ask each other questions, such as, "Is there anything that you need me to be doing that I'm not?" Or say, "Be honest. What do I do that you wish I didn't?" But it has to go both ways. Any question asked must also be answered, so that one person isn't feeling attacked. You may not like what you hear, but being aware is the best place to start. Most marriages that end in divorce ultimately do so due to unhappiness and resentment toward each other.

Bottom line is, you wouldn't expect to move up in your career without working hard and putting in the hours, or reach your fitness goals without working hard and eating right. So you certainly can't expect to have a happy marriage without working hard and communicating. Some couples like to renew their wedding vows every ten years or so, because they are different people now then they were then. To me, any excuse to buy a new dress and throw a party is a good idea that I fully support! But seriously, the first time most people get married they recite the predetermined words of the efficient. I know I did. Writing down your thoughts and feelings and then saying them out loud in front of your closets friends and family can be intimidating. But maybe that vulnerability is what makes the vows real, and allows the words to carry more weight. Or start out small by taking the time to hand write the messages in each others birthday cards each year, and go from there.

Vote for Jillian!

I can still remember my campaign for student council in seventh grade, when running for class vice president. It was *The Brady Bunch* theme, but I'm not quite sure why, considering it was about twenty years past the show's prime. Maybe I was trying to be retro? Anyway, it obviously didn't work, because I didn't win. I must have gotten over it though because I still ran for vice president of my sorority in college, but this time I won! If you've ever been on student council, involved in Greek life, or on a board of some sort, then you are familiar with the various positions, or roles, that need to be represented in order for things to run smoothly. I never realized it at the time, but the dynamics of a family unit run in a very similar yet unspoken way.

- **President**
  This person generally acts as the CEO (chief executive officer) of the household but is not necessarily the breadwinner. He/she might even be referred to as the one who "wears the pants" in the family.

- **Vice president**
  This person generally goes with the flow of things but is a great right-hand person. He/she steps up when needed and helps out with day-of execution.

- **Treasurer**
  This person runs the finances of the household. He/she makes sure the bills are paid on time, ensures the taxes get turned in, and probably checks the bank account and credit card statements on a regular basis. This person is usually, but not always, also the breadwinner of the household.

- **Secretary and public relations**
  This person gets the mail, RSVPs to parties, and runs the family calendar. He/she will buy the gifts, call extended family members just to say hi, or mail flowers when someone has fallen ill or just had surgery. They make sure there is always back-up toilet paper in the house, order the holiday cards on time, and get them in the mail before the first snowfall. He/

she makes sure everyone's hair is trimmed, clothes fit well and are clean, and home decor is up to date.

- **Programming and social chair**
  This person is in charge of planning the birthday parties, schedules adult dinner dates with other couples, blocks out time for family vacations, and initiates playdates with other kids. He/she makes sure the family social calendar always has something exciting to look forward to and that more fun memories will be created.

Since there are five chairs to be filled and usually only two adults running a household, naturally, each person will be holding more than one position. They say that opposites attract, and now you know why. If both people want to be treasurer, for example, someone is bound to lose unless roles are clear. If no one wants to be social chair, life can get dull and feel mundane. Every yin needs a yang.

Adulting Is Hard

My mother didn't have the luxury of having a mom while being a mom. In fact, it's something most adults with living parents probably take for granted. No one really thinks about it, but being a daughter as a child is obligatory, while being a daughter as an adult is more of an active choice. Your first eighteen years or so, you need your parents for survival and guidance. But as an adult, the relationship gradually shifts and takes on a slightly different role. Divvying up holidays and sharing time commitments evenly can be tricky. Sometimes you don't really want their advice, just a judgment-free sounding board to vent or complain to because you know they will love you unconditionally. Our parents probably still want to be reminded that they're appreciated. But as an adult with so many other responsibilities, sadly it ends up just being more of an unspoken understanding. The card companies have tried to help us all out by creating forced days of the year to spend five dollars on a folded piece of card stock, ten dollars on a box of assorted chocolates, or fifteen dollars on a bouquet of flowers. But isn't that a little like when we force a kid to say that they're sorry? It definitely means more if they do it on their own accord, and using their own words. I mean, who knows more about making grown-up decisions than the very grown-ups who raised us? Trial and error is great and all, but sometimes we just need to put our egos aside and ask for help. No shame in that game. Adulting is hard.

I Want to Be *That* Aunt

Everyone has that special aunt or uncle who either taught you how to drive, watched you while you parents were out of town, got you out of a jam, helped you land your first real job, or spent too much money on something just because they wanted to make you smile.

My great-uncle Leon was *that* uncle to many people. He was so special, in fact, that my husband and I wanted our son to carry on his legacy by sharing his name. I recently flew back to my hometown in Indiana to spend some time with him before he passed away, because his health had just taken a drastic turn for the worse. My flight got in on a Friday evening, and we drove directly to his home to be by his side. A hospital bed and a friendly hospice nurse had taken residency in the middle of his living room, and family members were surrounding him on the sofas and chairs that flanked my frail, dying uncle. This was a low experience on the seesaw for sure. He suffered from emphysema and COPD due to more than fifty years of smoking cigarettes every day. He owned it though. "I did this to myself," he often used to tell people when he would be hacking up a lung or had an oxygen tube in his nose to help him breathe. He would tell me to never start smoking and then would proceed to take an enormous inhale from his own lit cigarette. It was his Achilles' heel. His one bad vice. The addiction he just couldn't shake. And it ultimately stole years from his life, hundreds of thousands of dollars from his bank account, and precious time away from his friends and family when he would go outside by himself to get his fix. Was it really worth it? I can't imagine that the ends actually justified the means.

But there we were, six of us (seven, if you count the nurse, or eight if you count the three-pound guard dog perched at his feet) surrounding him in the comfort of his own home. We silently cried tears of love and sadness as we reminisced, ate, drank, laughed, and took turns holding his hand. We literally watched him take his very last breath of life. It sounded different from all of his previous inhales, which were labored and crackly. This one was almost clear, deliberate, and slow. There was a long pause, then a very intentional exhale that seemed to last forever. No one spoke. No one moved. You could hear a pin drop. He took one more clear breath, a bit smaller this time, and then the final exhale must have been so slow and shallow that it couldn't even be seen or heard by any of us. But that was it. After what felt like several minutes of anticipating a third breath but also knowing there wouldn't be one, I wiped away my steady stream of tears and instinctively (due to years of watching various doctor shows) looked at my watch. Time of death: 10:37PM Just like that, right before my very eyes. It was the most beautiful and peaceful thing I have ever witnessed. It was nothing like what I had seen in the movies or on TV though. There was no loud "beeeeeeeep" coming from a heart rate monitor, because there wasn't one. There was no hysterical parent or child collapsing to their knees while screaming in agony, because he didn't have living parents and never had any children. There was no hand-to-the-chest moment from the dying man trying desperately to cling to life, because he was ready to die. He had lived a full, rich, beautiful life and was now at peace. It was truly his time to go, and we all knew it, even him.

He was the epitome of what an extended family member should be— supportive and encouraging of your dreams and nonjudgmental of your mistakes. He was generous in times of need and caring in times of suffering. He always answered the phone when I called, and I could hear his smile through his voice, which instinctively always made me smile. Watching someone take their last breath will naturally make you think about your own mortality and what kind of an impact you will have on others, even long after you're gone. I hope that, in time, I can be *that* aunt to my adorable nephews.

"Hi, my name is _____"

So whether you're somebody's mom, wife, daughter, or aunt, make the highs on the seesaw with them extra high and appreciate the brief holds at the top. Because everyone knows that what goes up must come down, and your family is at the core of it all.

To help defuse the stubborn family bomb!

Girl Wash Your Face by Rachel Hollis: Yes, this is a self-help, motivational, female empowerment book. But I found the content about her family dynamics to be the most inspiring. My take away of her relationships with her small-town parents, big-city boyfriend/now husband, the tear jerking adoption story, and being a successful working mom of four kids, is what really wowed me. Girl, let's be friends!

book club

DISCUSSION QUESTIONS

Who is a family member that you admire and why?

_____

_____

How can you become *that person* to someone else in your own family?

_____

_____

What are the council positions you currently hold? Are there any that you would like to resign from, and what are the steps to making that happen?

_____

_____

chapter 5

FAITH BOMB

"Coincidence is God's way of remaining anonymous."

-Albert Einstein

I'm often caught off guard by the questions I've received over the years from my now 7-year-old son. One of which was, "mommy, what is faith?" To which I replied, "hmmm, I guess it's the opposite of doubt." And that lead to "what is doubt" etc., etc., you get the point. Whether you identify with a certain religious belief or not, there is a spiritual dimension to all of us that carries a sense of wonder for grasping life's purpose that simply cannot be denied. Spirituality can be found through many different ways—organized prayer, personal meditation, journal writing, or confiding in a trusted friend, just to name a few. In an effort to be all-encompassing and nondenominational, I'm going to refer to this spiritual mind-set as your "namaste." Being able to fully grasp your own understanding of what namaste means to you is an integral part of being able to defuse the five F-bombs. Just as you would start a five-hundred-piece puzzle by first completing the frame, think of namaste as your frame. It will make everything else fall into place much easier.

Many people have the wrong idea of what namaste truly represents. By default, you may conjure up an image of a vegan hippie who doesn't wear deodorant, is always smiling, and is probably listening to Phish music. Namaste. Or a die-hard yogi with a hemp "om" necklace on and her hair in braided pigtails. Namaste. Or a guy playing his guitar under a tree while sporting dreadlocks. Namaste. Hopefully I can prove you wrong.

They say that babies, cats, and dogs can feel your energy. They can sense when someone near them is nervous, anxious, or on edge and will instinctively start to cry, hiss, or bark in response to that negative energy, or what I'm going to call "lack-of-namaste." When a driver decides to ride your bumper, speeds past you, and then flips you off, you can choose between two options: (1) allow their lack-of-namaste to be contagious and yell right back, honk your horn, cry like a teenage girl, or do whatever nonproductive thing you can think of in that moment; or (2) you can choose to allow the peace that is within *you* to radiate positive energy their way, and thus *they* become more grounded and centered. Try it for one week, just for fun. What's the worst thing that could happen? Think back to a negative experience and play out what you might do differently next time to create a better outcome, should the situation occur again. This way, you'll be prepared to react to it more calmly.

It doesn't have to apply to just road rage; it could be any charged situation. The coworker who snaps at you, the child who throws a temper tantrum in the middle of a store, or the relative on the phone who thinks you wronged them—literally anything! Instead of letting their lack-of-namaste permeate into your cells and thus sink to their level, I challenge you to change their energy by throwing a big, heaping pile of namaste their way by smiling, taking a deep breath, and killing them with kindness. You will be shocked at how well this really can work. The coworker will feel like an ass for being so rude, the child will forget why they were hysterical in the first place, and the family member will hang up not remembering what you said but rather remembering how you made them feel. This ancient Sanskrit word is primarily used as a greeting and gesture of respect. It is often said in conjunction with the palms being pressed together in front of the chest and a slight bow of the head. My take on the meaning is, "May the peace that is within me greet and honor the peace that is within you."

When you are at peace, you tend to make smarter food choices, live a more active lifestyle, have better friendships, closer family relationships, and ultimately feel one with the universe. Believe me when I tell you that I had 14 jobs during the first four years after college. They ranged from various costume shops, to retail, waiting tables, retail, an administrative assistant, an assistant buyer at a corporate office, retail, sales for a grocery delivery service, teeter totter, teeter totter, teeter totter, and then I finally found my work namaste -- Pilates! Sure there have been some obstacles to overcome at different studios or with certain clients, but I always felt like I was where I was supposed to be in that moment. Yes, I eventually got the career that my heart knew I wanted. If you're not there yet, keep pushing your feet in the ground to propel you back up. You just gotta have faith!

Faith and Trust Go Hand in Hand

When you step onto an airplane, you trust the pilot and the aircraft to get you from point A to point B in one piece. The pilot is usually a person that you've never met, and the aircraft is basically a giant flying school bus that most of us can't actually comprehend the mechanics behind. But why should we trust them, and more importantly, why do we put our lives in someone else's hands so frequently and so freely? I'll tell you why. We have faith in the staff, and we have faith in the checks and balances system that has been put in place for our safety. Sure, some people may have an actual phobia of flying, but this example could be used in regard to an ER doctor, the chef cooking your food at a restaurant, the other drivers on the road, anything. You can't go through life not being able to trust people, at least to some extent. Always using common sense first, of course, you just have to have faith that others will treat you the same way you would treat them if the roles were reversed.

Feeling Gratitude

My friend Jenn and I were working out at our favorite little gym on the first Monday in January (along with everyone else) when my hamstring cramped up so badly that I stopped midexercise and immediately began stretching it while everyone else chugged along doing their kettlebell squats. I modified all my exercises the rest of the class. I normally felt euphoric when I left this particular workout, because I knew I kicked butt, but not that day. I was annoyed that my left hamstring felt like a piece of leather hide being pulled over a drum, and disappointed in myself that I didn't get in as great of a workout as I thought I should have. As I was feeling deflated, I suggested we pop into Peet's Coffee next door before going about our day. The first person I saw upon entering was an elderly man in a wheelchair with no legs. NO LEGS! He was smiling, enjoying his coffee and his conversation with his wife, and looking content. My heart got the message instantly. It was as if God was saying, "Quit your bitching lady, at least you have legs!" That's what I told myself anyway, and the seesaw popped right back up with great speed.

Trust Your Decisions

Thirty-seven is my lucky number, and it has been ever since I was ten years old. I've always known that I was going to have a huge thirty-seventh birthday party and that I would have my Bat Mitzvah on that weekend. And guess what? I did, and it was a magical experience in every possible way. When I would mention that I was studying for an adult Bat Mitzvah, I found people's reactions to be very surprising and usually not at all encouraging. The complete look of shock and confusion was almost priceless. The way I saw it, when you're between ten and thirteen years old, you're not making many decisions for yourself. You're told to go to school and when to go to bed. You can't drive yourself anywhere, and you can't earn your own money. You're just going through life blindly following your parents' orders with trust in the system because that's how it was done for them and so on and so forth. When I was ten years old, my parents actually asked me if I wanted to have a Bat Mitzvah when I turned thirteen. I said, "no," and that was the end of it. In that moment, I actually made my own decision, and I stand by it to this day. I truly believe I wasn't ready then. It needed to be on my own terms. Fast-forward to adulthood. I'm no longer a preteen trying to fit in and make good grades. I'm now a wife, a mother, and a fitness professional. I'm responsible for my own actions, and I get to make all my own decisions, because that's the way the system works. But what if it didn't work that way? What if you got to choose your own religion as a child? As it turns out, this is what our future is leaning toward after all.

What does a "normal" family look like, anyway?

Thanks to popular hit TV shows like *Modern Family, This Is Us, Will and Grace*, and *Grey's Anatomy* (just to name a few), today's culture has become more exposed to families that are not so nuclear. Viewing relatable scenarios with same-sex couples and interracial families has shown people that at the end of the day, we're all just human beings. Yes, we are all trying to defuse the same F-bombs to get through another day, and interfaith families are no exception. I have a large number of friends who were raised a different faith from that of the life partners they chose to marry and have kids with. When I've asked them about what religion they're going to raise their kids, the most common response has been, "We'll expose them to both and let them decide when they're old enough." I'm still not quite sure how all of this will play out in the end, but I'm eager to watch their decisions unfold. My guess is that the kids will choose to go with the religion of their closest friends, their favorite parent, or the one that is the most fun. But maybe not. Maybe the exposure will be thought-provoking enough for a developing mind to make an actual educated decision that feels like a good fit for their individual lifestyle.

My grandmother MaryAnn, a proud Episcopalian, told my dad before he converted to Judaism that as long as he believed in a "higher power," she fully supported his decision. I never grew up feeling like she disapproved of us or our belief system, and for that I am very grateful. Interfaith families can, and do, coexist every single day, regardless if they choose to believe in the same theory of how we all got here or where we're going in the end. And that's because the middle, the right now (the peanut butter and jelly), is the good stuff. Yes, the PB&J is supported by two pieces of bread, which are necessary to hold the delicious ingredients together. Let's refer to these slices of bread as the past and the future. By being in the present moment, you are choosing to be the peanut butter and jelly, the best part of the sandwich. No kid ever says they want to take two pieces of bread to school with nothing in the middle. Whatever's in the middle is always the best part.

Studies repeatedly show that living in the past will likely make you a more depressed person, because—let's be honest—you can't change what's already happened. Replaying a conversation in your mind won't change the ending, or dwelling on an accident won't undo it, and therefore serves no real purpose. But like it or not, the past has helped us to become who we are today. We are not defined solely by what has happened to us in our lives (the things we cannot control) but rather by how we have chosen to react to them. There is always a way to change your path in life. It is not written in stone. There's always a fork in the road or another option to choose. You just have to be open to seeing it, willing to find it, and brave enough to take it. Forgiveness doesn't mean admitting that what was done was okay. It means accepting that what was done cannot be changed.

On the flip side, someone who is living in the future is often in a constant state of assuming worst-case scenarios. This overthinker is living in a land of what-ifs, always waiting for the other shoe to drop, so to speak. This type of thinking can cause extreme anxiety and even lead to obsessive compulsiveness, lowering your quality of life. You could, however, use the thought of the future wisely to realistically set goals you want to achieve. Create a bucket list, for example, and fill it with places to see, things to do, or people to meet. Which brings us to Alice, the beloved character in a popular Disney story. This dreamer in Wonderland stepped right through the looking glass and ended up in quite a magical place indeed. She reminds us that every adventure requires a first step. And yes, all who wander are not necessarily lost. Always be curious, question authority, and don't waste time, as the present moment is what's most important.

Make Good Choices

This isn't anything you don't already know. But sometimes—don't deny it—your common sense takes little catnaps in the background of your brain. This is probably when the seesaw has hit the dirty ground. Attending a spiritual service can wake it up again and bring your common sense back to the foreground of your brain. Maybe you'll leave services feeling a bit lighter or refreshed and part of a community. Did you learn anything brand-spanking-new? Probably not. But it's a feeling of spiritual support to overcome whatever obstacle is facing you in life in that moment—an emotional pat on the back, if you will, a reminder that you're not alone in this big world and you've got this! And the seesaw goes back up.

Books I recommend to help defuse the stubborn faith bomb!

Spirit Junkie by Gabrielle Bernstein: I mean, "spirit" is literally in the title of this one, so it's not surprising that it might be a bit spiritual. But the juxtaposition of a "junkie" combined with the playful book cover displaying a graffiti art wall and the author in a hippie dress made me very intrigued, and her words definitely did not disappoint.

You are a Badass by Jen Sincero: "How to stop doubting your greatness and start living an awesome life" doesn't sound like it would be a book based around faith, so I was pleasantly surprised by the deliciously faithful content I found hiding inside the cover. This woman is a legit badass, and oh yeah, apparently so am I!

To Heaven and Back by Dr Mary Meal: I know what you're thinking, a medical doctor believes in science, research, and facts, period. But if you ever find yourself wondering about the afterlife, this boom should be on your short list. Her personal experiences are few and far between anything I've ever read about, especially the loss of her son... wow!

book club

DISCUSSION QUESTIONS

What does faith or namaste mean to you?

_____

_____

> "I honor the truth of who you are, which is a unique vibration of love."
> —Vanessa Johnson (yoga instructor)

> "Connected by the light in each of us."
> —Deb Reardon (yoga practitioner)

What is an example of a time you were able to change someone's mood for the better simply by sharing your positive energy?

_____

_____

If you created your own religion, what might you call it? What do's and don'ts would it have and what celebrity would likely be a member?

_____

_____

conclusion

RECESS ISN'T OVER!

Have Fun on the Playground

"You're never too old to try something new" is easier said than done. Years ago, I *tried* to do a bike ride excursion down Haleakala in Maui, Hawaii. In theory, it was a really great idea. They picked us up at our hotel at five o'clock in the morning in a rickety old van and drove us to the very top of an active volcano. They provided the bikes, helmets, and jumpsuits to wear over our clothes, and we just had to follow the tour guide (on said bike) down the edge of the enormous volcano while the van slowly followed behind. Except that's not how it went down for me. Nope. I had my very first, very real panic attack. One minute I was perfectly fine, excited to watch the sunrise over the Pacific Ocean with the wind on my face. And the next minute, it hit me like a ton of bricks. *This is a terrible idea* was now pulsating through my mind. As I was on my bike, gazing over the edge of this extremely large volcano, there were no guardrails and no bike lanes, just one road slightly wider than a car's width that we had to share with all the drivers. My throat began to close up, my eyes welled with tears, my hands instantly got clammy, and I felt like I couldn't breathe. I got off the bike almost as quickly as I had gotten on it. I didn't feel like I held the remote control to my own body. It was almost like someone or something else had taken it and changed all of my internal programming. Any sense of rationale went right out the window. I was 100 percent certain that if I got back on that bike, I would be entering my inevitable death while tumbling down the side of Haleakala. No ifs, ands, or buts about it. Death was clearly the only option here. My seesaw was so low it was indenting the lava rock below me. I ended up riding back down in the rickety old van while I watched everyone else on the excursion enjoying the wind in their faces, just like on the brochure. In hindsight, I should have practiced a form of meditation to get through this panic attack, but at the time, I didn't know how to find my om.

Finding *Your* Om

Start by creating a relaxing space, or find a unique place that speaks to you in a calming or meditative way. This could be as simple as a porch swing in your backyard or as grand as the sprawling banyan tree in Maui. This tree has become my om no matter where my life takes me. The tree is currently located across the street from the Lahaina Courthouse on Front Street but was originally imported from India in 1873. It is now the size of an entire city block and stands more than sixty feet high. I went to this spot with my son over winter break so he could practice journal writing. We found a dirty, handmade bench to sit on while enjoying our sticky ice-cream cones in the cool shade provided by the massive tree surrounding us like a dome. From there, we took in all the various sounds. Some were coming from the man sitting cross-legged on the sidewalk, playing his guitar, hopeful to make a few bucks. Others were from the waves crashing in the ocean nearby, but most were from the birds of all sizes and colors that were singing sweet songs to one another. Every inch of this tree that was reachable by human hands was filled with carvings of people's initials, either confessing their love for each other or just an ego wanting to leave its mark, making sure the world knew they had been there. There were dates and names carefully etched into this ancient tree, as if it was a monstrous tombstone in a graveyard. People watching could have been an Olympic sport here. French, Spanish, Hebrew, Chinese, English, you name it, were being spoken all around us. Faces smiling for smartphones or expensive cameras, fingers holding up peace signs, kids refusing to smile on the count of three, the typical tourist scene of family scenarios from across the globe. I was taking it all in, drinking it up like the last bit of hot chocolate after a long day of skiing, not wanting to miss a single drop. As I watched the birds trotting about in hopes of eating bits of food left behind from the visitors, the smell of the salt air was taking over our nostrils, and all our senses were engulfing the surroundings. The roots took on lives of their own—each one with a uniquely intertwined family but still connected to its Mother Earth through various wooden umbilical cords that hung from above like a huge pergola strung with holiday lights. The beauty was so palpable that I don't have to actually be back there to feel it again. I can now use the memory of my experiences to transport myself to that incredible tree and become grounded. You too can borrow from your own favorite memories and sit in silence, with your eyes gently closed, while taking long, slow, deep breaths in through the nose and then exhaling back out through the nose. As your thoughts begin to drift away from your current stressors or worries, they will transport you to a new, more peaceful state of mind.

If you can't think of a memory that you want to recreate, try counting the seconds it takes to reach your full inhale, and then match the same number of seconds on the exhale. Or if there is a stressful situation that is currently on your mind, come up with a short positive mantra to say in your head. For example, "I know the information. I will pass the test tomorrow," as opposed to a negative mantra like, "I will not fail the test tomorrow." Even though they are both essentially saying the same thing, in the negative mantra, your brain will be hearing the word "fail" on repeat and is now subconsciously expecting to fail. Instead, keep repeating the positive mantra with the word "pass" over and over again, and before you know it, you should be meditating! You can come up with your own default mantra to use on a daily basis and then change it occasionally to fit whatever life has thrown at you. Anyone remember the old *Saturday Night Live* bit called "Daily Affirmations with Stuart Smalley"? He would gaze into his mirror and say, "I'm good enough, I'm smart enough, and dog-gonnit people like me." We all got a good laugh out of his positive outlook on life, but maybe he's the one who had it right all along.

I know that, for example, when I'm using a credit card machine and it clearly states, "Do Not Remove Card" I instinctually always want to remove the card! My brain chooses to ignore the "Do Not." I wish that it would just tell me what TO do, "Keep Card Inserted" instead of what NOT to do. I can't seriously be the only one who thinks this, right? Prime example; when I want my son to stop running in circles,

I don't tell him to stop running in circles because it's dangerous and he can hurt himself or others. In fact, that only makes him want to run even more. Instead, I tell him, "I bet you can't stand on one foot for a minute" and the next thing I know he's trying to stand on one foot! Circles averted. When I took my yoga teacher training course in L.A. a few years ago, there were only 9 students in the class. Each and every morning for fourteen consecutive days, we all had to take turns and lead the class in a Sun Salutation. Our instructor would constantly remind us not to start with, "Ok, so, first we're gunna…" and then low and behold, every single person would start with some version of "Ok, so, first we're gunna" and they would immediately catch themselves, or we would all call them out on it… Every. Single. Time! So before I went, I repeated in my head "Thank you for joining me today, lets begin by stepping to the front of our mats…" and then that's exactly what came out of my mouth.

"Praying is the time to ask and meditating is the time to listen."
-Gabrielle Bernstein

If meditation is not your thing, that's okay! Many people use music to help quiet their mind. Create a playlist on your phone so that you are able to quickly access songs that help you find your om. Some people feel more centered when they're playing an instrument, painting, crafting, reading a magazine, lighting a candle, deleting emails, taking a walk without a cell phone, sitting in a massage chair, or even just being outside in the sunshine. These solo moments are ways to recharge your energy the same way you would recharge your phone when it falls to less than 10 percent before the day is actually over. They can be done spontaneously, inexpensively, and quickly. When you find what works for you, schedule it as a standing repeat event in your calendar. If you do need to recharge, take comfort in knowing that the time is already carved out for you to do so, and if you don't, just skip it that day!

My hope is that your thought, word, and deed will all be aligned. Yoga teaches us that if you only think positive thoughts, you will only speak kind words and therefore only have good actions. So what are you waiting for? Write down your goals, talk about them with others, and see them happen in real life. Because at every age, especially as women, we deal with our own F-bombs every day while still enjoying the crazy ups and downs on the seesaw of life.

- You know that you need to be eating the right foods to fuel your body properly and to eliminate the ones that make you sluggish.
  Food bomb

- You know that you need to move your body more often if you want it to work *for* you and not *against* you.
  Fitness bomb

- You know that you need to have a good friend or a group of girlfriends who support you and that you can rely on in times of need.
  Friend bomb

- You know that you need to embrace the various aspects of your family members, no matter how crazy they may be.
  Family bomb

- You know that you need to trust the unknown and learn to calm the mind.
  Faith bomb

There's no way you can defuse all of these bombs all the time. But you do your best, you outsource when you need to, you learn from your mistakes, and you grow. Some days are better than others, but the ride on the seesaw sure is fun.

about the author

JILLIAN POTASHNICK

Jillian has been teaching Pilates in Las Vegas since 2008 and has been a kids' yoga instructor since 2016. She has completed courses in TRX, Gliding, PiYo, two-hundred-hour yoga teacher training, W.I.T.S. personal training, Pilates Method Alliance, and more. She has been featured on the *Fit Fierce and Fabulous* podcast (episode 67) discussing the importance of good posture. She is proud to be a Fabletics Style ambassador for the Las Vegas Downtown Summerlin location. She was interviewed on the importance of functional fitness for *Pilates Style* magazine (page 77) in the November/December 2016 issue.

For daily "fitspiration," follow her on Instagram @1109fitness.

Jillian's YouTube channel, *1109 Fitness*, is designed for those of you who don't have time to fit a full hour of training into your busy day. It offers a variety of workouts that range from four minutes to twenty-two minutes, usually consisting of only one hundred reps. The idea is to fatigue the muscles, then keep going. After all, if it doesn't challenge you, it doesn't change you. For best results, do these strength-training videos in conjunction with cardio and good nutrition for a strong and healthy body!

many thanks

Thank you to all of my amazing clients for allowing me to be a part of your lives over the years and for entrusting me to help you reach your fitness goals

Thank you to my very creative and talented sister, Evelyn Bark @ honestlypaperie, for the clever artwork and graphic designs made especially for *The Five F-Bombs*.

Thank you to my fabulous beta readers for your tremendous help in the execution of this book: Audrey Kelly, Dr. Danielle Richards, Deb Reardon, Deirdre Ezra, Ingrid Lewis, Jennifer Vonderahe, Dr. Jordyn Trockman, Kala Flynn, Kelly Davis, Kendra Forney, Libby Pass, Liz Auten, Rachel McArdle, Sara Shaughnessy, and Teri Lachman.

Without all of these fantastic people in my life, this book would not have come to fruition.

CPSIA information can be obtained
at www.ICGtesting.com
Printed in the USA
BVHW030927120819
555663BV00008B/90/P

9 781982 232535